ALSO BY JAMES L. HARTER SR.

Mindsongs: Chapter One

Heartfelt Thoughts: Chapters Two & Three
Mindsongs/Treks
Mindsongs/Strolling

Heartfelt Thoughts: Chapters Four & Five
Mindsongs/Wayfarer
Lifesongs

Heartfelt Thoughts: Chapters Six & Seven
Preface to Life
Life Goes on

Heartfelt Thoughts: Chapters Eight & Nine
Glimpses of Life
Catching Up

Heartfelt Thoughts

Chapters Ten and Eleven

James L. Harter Sr.

Heartfelt Thoughts Chapters Ten & Eleven by James L. Harter Sr.
Copyright © 2014 by James L. Harter Sr.

Cover design and layout by Alexandra King

Heartfelt Thoughts Chapters Ten & Eleven by James L. Harter Sr.
122p. ill. cm.
ISBN 978-1-935795-34-6

All Rights Reserved. No part of this book may be reproduced, stored in a retrieval system, or transmitted in any form or by any means, electronic, mechanical, photocopying, recording, or otherwise, without permission in writing from MRK Publishing

MRK Publishing
PO Box 353431
Palm Coast, FL 32135-3431

Printed in the United States of America

As ever an again, to my dear wife, Shirley

Contents

Chapter Ten: Seek Find

Preface 2
Day In, Day Out 3
Undo Katy 4
Now I lay me down to dream 4
creation 5
Insights to Selfdom 6
Relief 7
Still Life Paintings: 1 8
                                     2
                                     3
ripple down 9
Endless Love 10
Times like these 11
Rhapsody in Black 12
Just everything 13
venting 14
Wouldn't it be wonderful if 14
An Entry into Prose Number Seven: The Wanderer 15
From the Prayer Book 16
An Entry into Prose, Number Eight: The Recall 17
Like clicking footfalls on a tile floor 19
Spirits in the Wind 20
Reflections on a Garden Pool 21
Snailspace 21
The Outlook 22
A Society Bent on Civil Conflict 23
Earthworks 23
Look up, Look out, Look in 23
Oxymoronic Sanity 24

Nightbeat 25
An Entry into Prose Number Nine: The Big Secret 26
one task 27
Oh mind of mine, where is thy sting? 27
Setting Sights, Setting Sails 28
Punchdrunk 29
A Tale in Prose: Ole' Buck 30
Counterpoints 31
Potpourri 32
Time In, Time Out 33
Musings   I 34
         II
         III
         IV
Remains of the Day 35
Tranquility 35
I ambiance 36
back soon 37
Knightfall 37
The Leaving 39
here and there 39
The Prince of Light 40
A Fawn . . . A Child 40
Good Goose Rhymes   1 41
                    2
                    3
                    4
Lepidoptera Magic 42
easy come, easy go 43
Trails 43
Gabriel's Windsong 44
Rodin on the Shelf 46
Degrees of the Heart 46

burnout   47
re-entry   47
The Waiting Game   47
Proof Positive Times Four: 1   48
                              2
                              3
                              4

The Beginning   49

Chapter Eleven: On On Moving On

Preface   52
Emergence   53
Flight of the Bumbling Pea   54
Sucking Our Freedom Away (SOFA)   55
Only Yesterday   56
Seeing the Bud in a New Light   57
Foxfire   57
when creative juices flow   58
The Question   59
The Touch   60
etchings on a leaf   60
The Cicada Brief   61
Suess Land: Mired in "Tock Sick" Waste   62
The Outlook   62
Rise and Shine   63
Venues   65
Hold that Thought   65
Exit Right   66
Playwright   67
Who Cares?   68
daffodils in freeze   69

alone in silence   69
Moon's Caper   70
Fancies   70
The Last Supper   71
Rockwellian Americana   71
Dream Flight   72
Hello! Who's there?   73
Sorry, this lion is busy   73
Fleeting Melancholia   74
Putting a Stop to the Blues   75
Delta Force   76
Dancing with Clouds   77
Whither Samaritans, do ye go?   78
Court Sense   79
Some Cheap Shots   80
Something wicket this way comes   81
A Sense of Purpose   82
Ponder   83
Dewdrop Tinctures   83
When Dreams Become You   84
Sometimes   84
Something about Nothing   85
From This Day Forward   86
Whose hands are these?   88
All that I have   89
Who   90
Prelude to a Munich Fest   91
Majestic Enrapture Capture   92
Taking the Time to Rhyme   94
Permutations and Lamentations   95
The Mystery of Myself   96
Life   97
Pie in the Sky   98

Heaven Lea   100
The Dawning   101
A Poet's Task   102
The Silhouette   102
The Sentinel   102
Chalk Talk in a Blackboard Jungle   103
1. Little Miss Muffed It   103
2. All Sewn Up   103
3. Fork It   103
Hell's Afire   104
The High and Mighty   104
Birds of a Feather   104
The Surge   105
Chalk Talk Flip Flop   106
Moving On Trilogy ...ONE: Glory Be!   106
                   ...TWO: Willow   107
                   ...THREE: We the People   108
Postscript   108
The Beginning   109

Chapter Ten:
Seek - Find

Preface

After over six hundred and twenty entries, I'm about to embark on this, my tenth book. I wonder if I will ever be totally drained of ideas or new insights. As long as I continue to seek my inner self and strive to find my internal universal love; then as long as I may live, the possibilities of ideas and new insights are endless. I still remain intrigued and desirous to achieve a complete oneness with my inner child. Everyone of us has the child within us, but not everyone has the desire or attitudinal interest to search and discover. Seeking and finding the experience, establishing natural communication and the fulfillment in being together; the kid and the adult is an embraceable effort destined to produce wondrous rainbows of love and contentment.

My sister-in-law, Mary, was recently working on a movement coining the word, Kidult. Her intent was to represent the very essence of seeking and finding the inner child within every human being, no matter the time or their station in life.

Just by bouncing a ball, hugging a tree, laughing gleefully, re-establishing an insatiable curiosity, accepting everything at face value with wonder, loving everything and dedicated learning,- always learning, could be a few of the countless roads leading you to the heart and soul of the child within each of us.

So let us go on, seeking and hopefully finding our inner peace, our inner love, our cherub of happiness, our Golden Child of eternal joy. Good journey!

Read and enjoy. Learn and explore with me. I'll be seeing you from time to time along the way.

Day in, Day out

Tangled webs of gnarling beauty
    sifting through the darkness
Creeping dawn's a weeping specter
    bringing in a freshness –
    new birth to eager eyes.

Can that which lies beyond be any better
    than that which has come this way before?
What I take for granted are the everyday miracles, -
    the masterpieces imaged on an old canvas.
Do I grow older with each image,
    none the wiser, if I just let them pass me by?
Standing there - watching the parade
    not marching in it
    not getting with it.

Caught in tangled webs of drudgery
    lazy eyes in swamps of boredom
    bogged, oh so bogged.

Open up! Feel the ever sculpted earth.
        Breath in each miracle.
        Revel in being alive.
        Love yourself.
        Be happy.

What comes next is better than before.

Undo Katy

Katydid what Katyduzz
if Katy didn't
there'd be no buzz
if buzz she didn't
then what Katyduzz
will ne'er be done
becuzz, becuzz

Now I Lay Me Down to Dream

in the eyes of drowsy cherubs
in the dreams of memory beds
in the hearts of snuggled pillows
amidst the folds of quilted spreads
lie the wondrous worlds of selfdom
wherein a boundless freedom treads
and the mighty self made heroes
cavort in dreaming tousled heads

Creation

a flower proud, stood strong and true
    a trumpet in the sky
but in short time fell sunset hills
    none came to die, to die

bare the heart, oh slay the squelch
    let the fingers play the tune
the thoughts inside burst forth a cry
    startling the tranquil moon

and soon the nightshade comes to life
    freeing the darkened eyes
the lightened heart gives rise to dawn
    though morning's in disguise

a flower proud, stands strong and true
    triumphant hues on high
the songs go forth in fervent stretch
    breathing in the eager sky

the blossom takes the giving sun
    accepting its full intent
and born this day in a vibrant heart
    is a message heaven sent

Insights to Selfdom

Don't search for the thorns in the person
    rather seek the blooms in their souls.

*****

Denying love is a walk in the dark.
Embracing love is a walk in the park.

*****

Orient a house on a site
    so that the rooms receive the right sunlight,
    and the interior will be loved by its dweller.
Do the same with your life,
    and you will love yourself.

*****

Hitler existed because there was no love
    in those lives which existed around him.

*****

Love is an elixir, - the oxygen for our soul.

*****

Eternity meets time only during this very moment.

*****

Two minds in conflict are universes unto themselves;
    while two in concert share no distance.

Relief

take no grief
in a fallen leaf
hued to the earth
crisp beauty down

take to heart
meld the hue to your soul
savor, revere
and your spirits will soar

take what is gained - sustained
a new life within
replenished and re-displayed
fresh green - come spring

Still Life Paintings

1

an oaken bucket brimmed with fallen rain
    sodden sides still liquid slick
        reflecting the rippled red rose
            entangled on the weathered wood
                of a knotty-pine split rail fence post

2

a lazy garden rake adorned with muddy tines
    framed by the flaxen pampas reeds
        the sinewy handle casually draped
            with a sweaty tattered denim shirt
                pink petunia peeking from a pocket

3

four felt-like fronds of frilly ferns
    bowing to greet a silky tawny toadstool
        all dew-laden in the dreamy dawning mist

Ripple Down

the arms of a comforting soul
embrace a saddened heart
teardrops ripple down
running over river rocks
eddies of thoughts are lost
in the rush of the maddening horde
pushed by a sodden frenzy
crushed by a latent greed
skipping the now
escaping the morrow
pushed, pushed
pushing, pushing
going, going to somewhere
going nowhere
teardrops lost to the sea
forgotten
ripple down once from a source
caught up in the force
pushed, going and gone

Endless Love

I love you in this time of ours
    a forever time of endless hours
I love you during this slashing strife
    You are my wings, you are my life
I love you though what I show may be
    a selfish silent dichotomy
I love you dearly and feel your grief
    Yet I have no words to give relief

What is in one's soul to be that silent
    am I that closed, so self reliant?
What do I do to bare heart and soul?
    Why am I left with just poetry?
To hold your hand still remains a thrill
    your soft skin still instills a chill
To see you dressed in clothes so fine
    hand picked, tasteful, always divine

I love you, Shirl, in that I duly know
    these words I've said have got to show
I love you more than the words I write
    What I've been saying is far from trite
I love you with all my heart and soul
    You are my life, you and I are whole
I love you in this time of hours
    a forever time of endless hours

Times Like These

what can be said of trying times
when thoughts are drained of bliss
when scheming swords cry freedom
yet are dripping, wrenched. a-twist
when the riots of forgotten people
lie lost, swamped in mire and murk
when smiles of sorrows wizened
mirror fearing faces of lives berserk

what can be said of trying times
when the hopes of shattered dreams
are scattered in some foreign land
where nothing but silence screams
when the souls of the lonely people
sulk inward deep in blackened caves
when the hearts of beaten drummers
are left bashing in pounding waves

what can be said of trying times
when spirits grasp for silken sky
and the gleams of joyful children
are blessed by a Christ child's cry
when the blooming minds of serfdom
revere the King of heaven's might
when all the joy and love within
embraces his ever- guiding light

Rhapsody in Black

in the mocking echoes of the night
    no dawn ascended
    and fear extended
shades and shadows of ebony delight

crystal tears left at a crying door
    through liquid pleasures
    and deceitful treasures
the governed mourn over a hollow war

heroes are born from those who obey
    no need for a reason
    no matter the season
yet in their homes they'd rather stay

Just Everything

take one day at a time
hold the hour in your hand
savor the minute
bless the second
and in an instant
life becomes eternity
your space is your universe
you touch infinity
and all that is about you
is also within you
and all that is within you
is unconditional love.
Love for: the sunbeam glow,
      the raindrop show,
      the breezes, the sloe-eyed doe,
      the snowflake, the icicle,
      the bubbly tot upon his tricycle,
      the rainbow, the stream in flow,
      the butterfly, the changing sky,
      the dawn, the dew, the mist,
      and a baby's tiny fist,
      excitement in your soul,
      a birthing spindly foal,
      tree rustle and bee hustle,
      friendly eyes and damsel flies,
      fuzz and silk and yellow roses,
      apple crisp and Grandma Moses,
      the star afar, the meadow grain,
      a life, your life, the bounding main,
      the firefly, the smiling dimple,
      and everything, just plain and simple.
Just everything.

Venting

bad gasses escape
through ducts defined
whether within our body
or in buildings designed

proper venting
allows the human mind
to release those gasses
which are maligned

Wouldn't it be Wonderful

oh, wouldn't it be wonderful if
    butterflies lived longer
    streets were void of snow
    we all were filled with glee
    and the homeless knew exactly where to go?

oh, wouldn't it be wonderful if
    my future was today and now
    I believe that I believe
    we all worked together
    and the world had not a thing to grieve?

An Entry into Prose Number Seven:
The Wanderer

Some say that automatic writing evolves from the mind-hand of an unseen spirit. Yet, others say that perhaps it comes from the subconscious depths of the living writer himself.

However, there may be, at the very least, another possibility. What dwells in the caverns of the human mind could conceivably be an embodiment of a universe of communicating souls. Our conscious mind has hardly even begun to tap the informational superhighway of our own subconscious.

The scientific and physiological reference to the subconscious may be a misconception; in that we believe that the subconscious mind is a tangible substance and is a physical part of our actual self. What could very well be the case; is that our subconscious is similar to a computer window; an opening to the cosmos, which is networking of thoughts, forever wandering and circulating in the vast expansive universe. If the human mind, which is basically always turned on, could also tune into these windows at will, then the network circuiting would be received as thoughts and ideas just as those which are now generated within the conscious mind. (That's a heavy paragraph).

(continues)

The soul is a wanderer, an intermediate, a translator, a giver, and a receiver of our consciousness. The soul is a communicator to God and to self. To love your self is to love God, and to love everything, everywhere unconditionally.

Someday, your self will be a part of your God, all as one entity in the universe.

Someday, you will be a wanderer too.

From The Prayer Book

> What's on your mind?
> What news have you prepared for me today?
> Let me hear you say what is in your heart today.
> I cannot seem to find a way to open myself up
>   to have a communication with you.
> Will you give me some clue as to how to
>   proceed?
> What must I do? Let's begin with a prayer.

Dear God:

I love you and all you represent but somehow I don't know how to communicate except for just talking. I guess that's all right. I have a need to find a new way in my life.

I don't know why I have no energy or the where-with-all to provide a productive and viable life for myself and all those around me. I need a new perspective on my career, and with my dear wife, and with my sexual relationship, and with my service to mankind.

    (continues)

I need your help, and I will do all I can to help you if some light is shed on how I am to proceed with the next step.

Please help me now.

Please offer me some direction.

Your servant,
James L. Harter, Sr.

An Entry into Prose Number Eight: The Recall

Plucking my expanding book from the shelves of time and whisking away the dust and cobwebs of neglect; I recalled a chapter or two of self enlightenment that, perhaps, might have been lost to me forever.

It's funny what trickles through the caverns of the mind. Sometimes I find the loveliest of memory pools of thought lying still - serene and waiting; waiting there for me . . .

I was a young lad, of some Mayan, Aztec, Toltec or Incan tribe, of which I know not. I was wearing a loin cloth of leather of some sort and a light moccasin- like foot covering. I was tan and svelte and had long dark hair. My eyes were alert and searching, for what I know not. How I arrived at this particular spot escapes my memory.

(continues)

The space was made entirely of rock, including the ceiling which appeared several stories above me. Light, coming from my left, was filtering through a massive stone checkerboard wall of squat rectangles of dark stone and white, bright light.

I could see the green of what seemed like a dense forest or jungle through and beyond the wall. Some sun appeared to be painting the largess of growth many shades of green. I was either, escaping from something or just exploring; doing what any young lad might do. I was scampering over large boulders and I remember stopping and pausing on one of the more flattened masses, feeling exhilarated and ecstatic. Why I was there, what I was doing, where I was going, what was going to happen next; I know not, and I wonder if I ever will.

That's all there is; at least for now. The whole bizarre episode remains so vivid in my conscious mind. This is the one and only recollection that I seem to remember and think about again and again and again.

Like Clicking Footfalls on the Tile Floor

I stand in the springtime of this perfect April day
Gathering in all the sights and smells of nature's play
    And wondering as I stand alone
      What new excitement is to come my way?
Then a lonesome clatter tone is all that I mind to hear

And, I start, as if some alien creature is about to
Pounce from some corner of my eye
    An ugly, unsteady
    Crab-like creature shifting sideways
      Its stalked beady-eyes and pincers at the ready
Again, a lonesome clatter tone pierces my watchful ear

And I twist about, feeling goose bumps in my heart
Adrenalin pushing me into an anticipating wary state
    Eyes flick and dart towards every point
    I spy nothing anywhere; - no ugly reprobate
Then, that lonesome clatter tone belongs to me again
    So near
Yester-autumn's maple tear, brown, dry and gnarled
    So crisp
Whisked by springtime gusts of warming flavor
    Scampers and clatters, stops and starts, all alone
    Chattering, clattering over the tarmac paver
That lonesome clatter tone is nothing but a leaf
    So mere

Spirits in the Wind

All those spirits in the wind, whither do they go?
There are spirits in the wind, blowing to and fro
The saga of a simple man
      lies somewhere in the frenzied flow
Seeds of time are borne aloft,
      delaying time to sprout and grow
While on earth a life is lived,
      yet so very little does it know
That not finding love and meaning;
      it will linger here below
There are spirits in the wind, blowing to and fro.
All those spirits in the wind, whither do they go?

Reflections of a Garden Pool

where upon looking into the flowing skies
    the golden carp cavort in cirrus guise
where water lilies burst into cumulous blooms
    a dragonfly hovers, then darts and zooms
where a meadowlark glides through the liquid blue
    and a water strider sports the indigo hue
where you genuflect to miracles
    in awe of His wondrous deeds
where you accept His love
    and plant His giving seeds
where when you are feeling down
    it is to this placid pool you go
knowing it's the perfect place
    where you will glow and grow

S   N   A   I   L   S   P   A   C   E

    to take up such a tiny space
        and move through time at such a pace
            the future becomes a far-off place
                more of now does he embrace
                    in any case, he's won life's race

The Outlook

I stand on the threshold of life and find that I have
    but three choices that I can make:

One
I can see what the weather is like and step back away from the threshold, shut the door and return to my hovelled existence. Sheltered from adversity, relishing the past and lying stagnant in the present; I never have any caring to face the future.

 Life is dead.

Two
I can stand upon the threshold; neither stepping out nor staying in. I know there is security in my past. I can stand here in the present and watch the world go by.

Life is boring.

Three
I can cross over the threshold; step out and embrace my future. The past is always an open door behind me, yet remains only memories. Each step is my presence and my present. My future is my horizon. All the paths before me become all the choices.

Life is exciting.

A Society Bent on Civil Conflict

too rich at the top
too poor at the bottom
and nothing in between
smash, clash, burning trash
power versus numbers
doomsday is foreseen

Earthworks

farmers of the soul
    till the ends of time
        sow the seeds of love
           and reap the benefits
              of the nourished heart

Look up, Look out, Look in

Look up. Your future is yours to be.
Look out. Your environment is yours to cherish.
Look in. Your self is yours for the learning
    and for the knowing.

Oxymoronic Sanity

suspended raindrops
scampering snails
destined ship's sails
    blow still on barren seas
blunders of calm rage
    escape frenzied trauma
    rioting into colorless rainbows of deliria
silence rampages from a gaggle of trumpets
    do we dare ponder the wind?
        that it pulses?   that it thrusts?

do we really care at all?
    society's treadmill molds immoral clay
    dismal flowers their vases display
humanity defiles humility; then festers in decay

yet, do we really care at all?
skunks wallow in their very own stench
    judges decree from their very own bench
paper dolls, snipped from sensual tabloids
    cavort in vogue before cosmopolitan androids

but, do we really care at all?
    life's waste is abundantly plundered
    holocausts are never-ending stories
    vultures and jackals have not forgotten

neither have we.

Nightbeat

Darkness is not a mystery or a death.
Darkness is not a fear.
Darkness is serenity of a different kind;
    One that sends the mind
           to ponder
           to wonder
           to be with oneself
                  to be there with the Great Alone
There is a light in the night of darkness
        a light of knowing
        a light of being
The trees' forest tops, in silhouette to the dusky sky
    Stand stoic; - knowing of the times
           knowing of the day
           knowing of my presence
And I, in turn;- am knowing of their presence
                knowing that we exist as one
I age with them
Sage with them
I grow with them
Glow with them.
We are the night
We are together.
We light the night in every way.
We are the heartbeat of the night.
We are the night-beat.
We live
We thrive
We are alive

An Entry into Prose Number Nine:
The Big Secret

All too often, during our growing years, we are taught to
". . . just grow up!" or "Don't be such a child!" and we listen and our youth is stolen and goes away. We get too busy in midlife with adult things; money, business, family crises, social competition and we are introduced to stress.
Youth has disappeared in us. We have forgotten the child that is within us and we have lost contact with our inner selves.

Have you ever wondered why there seems to be a mystic electricity between a tot and an elderly person? The elderly have taken the time to reflect and recall their youth, to embrace themselves and to face reality as it should be faced. Holding on to your inner child and embracing your soul is a wonderful experience and truly a gift that only YOU can be enthused about and only YOU can enjoy.

The Big Secret is to never lose sight of the "kid" in you. Be sensibly reckless, feel young, act young, and be yourself again.

Though it is extremely difficult to maintain a focus on oneself all of the time; lapses do occur which makes it easy to lose sight of oneself from time to time. The ability to come back to your self and to your inner child is both an accomplishment and a thrill.

I am glad that I am still a kid at heart.

One Task

suppose
I froze
or chose
to close
the door of my selfish id

I might
despite
my fright
delight
myself in what I just did

Oh Mind of Mine, Where is Thy Sting?

Begrudgingly bemoaning the fact that beneath the
benign thoughts of this bewildered soul, lies the
beguiling belief that beekeepers belaboring over bees
can beseechingly come to me before my eyes can seize
the sea of cee's dancing in the hieroglyphs of dee's and
ease and other runic thoughts besieging me.
Be gone, be gone, oh behemoth of letter culture!
Belittle me no more.
Let me choose to be when I bequeath and not before!

Setting Sights, Setting Sails

Destiny, oh destiny, my hand's upon your wheel;
Everything seems A-OK; we're on an even keel
When night befalls, bright Polaris is my sight
Is it I who guides you onward
    or is it you who steers me right?
A common place in space
    is what I'm destined to embrace
And yet it's unique to each of us within the human race
To stand upright, to be forthright
Unencumbered, one among the many
One with sight to see the light
Yet alone in thoughts, - in schemes
Alone to unravel mysterious mosaics
    of our fondest dreams
One Master Sculptor has molded all
    and yet has molded each
Left here on earth to struggle, grope
    and yet to stretch and reach
For the star afar, the golden fleece, or the holy grail
Knowing now my mighty ship has finally begun to sail
To the sea, then to the sea,
    the boundless eyes keep roaming
For an omen, any omen
    to which horizon I should be homing.
Destiny, oh destiny, my hand's upon your wheel
Everything seems A-OK; we're on an even keel
When night befalls, bright Polaris is my sight
Is it I who guides you onward,
    or is it you who steers me right?

Punchdrunk

count ten
and then
he says it's over
no recourse
unless of course
you dare
to go a-round again
same life
down and out
flat and broke
boos burning inside
hazy
dazy
crazy

count ten
oh, no not again
life bears
a bigger
better box
far better
than the ring within
begin with cheers
in your heart
be smart
depart
restart
love is a-bout
fight for it

A Tale in Prose: Old Buck

Ask anybody and they'll tell you 'bout Ole Buck sayin' he wuz the most ornery red-neck-ed cuss in these hare parts. None other could compare or dare to stare him down. Some swear it's 'cause his britches wuz too tight, others claim he wuz jest plain downright ornery. He had got hisself a mean streak deeper than that big rock canyon over yonder.

Shucks, I oughta knows 'cause he's my granpappy.

I recalls the time Ole Buck yelled a grizzley offen a mountin, spitten' in his snarlin' face, and then plumb scarin' the hide right offen that bear, jest by snarlin' back. Ole Buck sure was one ornery cuss.

The day before the Great Dust Storm, Ole Buck was chewin' Saguaro, chompin' on the needles like they wuz spaghetti. He tole me the storm was comin' and that he figured to snarl and stare it down. Yo never saw so many scared rabbits as we were, hide-tailin' it and a- runnin' for cover, diggin' holes; hunkerin' down in any pit we could muster.

But not Ole Buck, no siree. He stood his ground, makin' gosh darn awful noises, cussin' at the wind and snarlin' at the grit that rasped his wizened frame. Like stone bein' honed; he stood his ground. The wind blew and the dust flew, howlin' and whistlin' and raisin' a gosh darn awful ruckus all its own. The storm thundered into the past. Us scaredy cats poked up, and warily walked the parched and barren land. Nothin' was around and worst of all; there was nary a sign of Ole Buck, the ornery red-neck-ed cuss.

(continues)

To this very day,, this tale's bin tole a hunnert times plus more; of how Ole Buck, stood his ground and swore. They tell of his howlin' and whistlin' in the night.

They say; come full moon, Ole Buck is standing in the eerie light, eyes wild bright, starin' down the stubborn night. Trubble is, there's so many Ole Bucks out there; legend has it the storm rasped him into a zillion pieces. And all those pieces are standin' ground and starin' down each and every storm. They're standin' like red necks in the plain. They is today, so they say.

I's seen him too. He's standin' like a rock. I oughta knows' cause he's my granpappy.

Counterpoints

if each day you count your sorrows
    lamenting in past refrains
you cannot live for your tomorrows
    only haunting dark remains
for the Star of love and kindness
    brings warming rays to shine
let the joys and times of Christmas
    enthrall embracing hearts divine
come then and count your blessings
    sharing all your love with friends
all adorned in festive dressings
    receiving the messages it sends

Potpourri

Pastel scraps of forgotten trees
Crisp carapaces from thistle leas
Dried fragrance
Dyed.
Dormant, not dead
Waiting
    in a lonely, absent
    silent space; a nook
    a room, a lived-in place
Perhaps, a welcomed ambiance
I don't know why; nor do I know how
    sights and sounds seem keener now
New feelings
    spring from a derelict
    yet cozy corner
    of an awakened intellect
Wispy hints of lilac
    tingle my taunted nose
    or is it jasmine?
    oleander or yellow rose?
    is it ginger cinnamon or clove?
    nestled in this treasure trove
I sense another soul havened within this space
Perhaps a friend, a love
    a remembrance, or an embrace
So I crave and I give chase.
To seek and to find   Yet, no need   Never mind
These scraps are not forgotten trees
    but snips and sniffs of memories
Forevermore

Time in

Time out

Hi, small fry.
Don't fret.
Don't cry.
It's tick tock time.
It's tick tock rime.
Tock tick.
Watch the clock tick.
Hear the click tock.
Tick tock.
"Tick tock"
    mocks the clock.
"Tick tock"
Heck, hock the clock.
Tick tock song.
Tick tock gone.
Time to go too.
Oh, pooh
Boohoo.
Bye, old guy.
Sigh.
Hi, small fry.
Don't fret.
Don't cry.
It's tick tock time.

Musings

I   Turning the urn, a gilded fern
    blossoms from an ebon ogee form.
    What flowers will be held
    and smelled tomorrow?

II A porcelain boot, its kiln dried flowers
    bear not those who have trod,
    nor those who dare to trod
    in the footfalls
    of their soulful petals.

III A mighty yew
    gnarled in grizzled reality
    lets a playing sun
    gnarl it into yet
    a deeper mystery.

IV Castanets clacking
    stalking, talking to one other
    sleeping sombreros nod
    fiesta takes a siesta break

Remains of the day
I'm stumped. I'm stuck. I've not a clue.
Since the stump you see is nothing new
And yet each day the stump still stands
The stump stands still thru time's demands
But look deep in to its decaying matter
It is fodder plenty for an insect's platter

*****

The silent simplicity of quiescence
    brings images of unencumbered peace.

Tranquility

un-furrowed brow of a verdant grassy knoll
unruffled feathers of a stag horn fern
noncommittal swagger of an aspen leaf
nonplussed patience of a muted mum
soul baring depths of a placid pond
serene echoes lost in cobwebbed cushions
easy eyes inhaling the immobility of time.

chimney top swirls join morning misty curls
yawning throats of strewn empty barrels
staunch picket sentinels circle garden rows
stalwart granite heroes staring in frozen emotion
still life portraits within a sleepy city-scape
bustling echoes lost in moth-balled monoliths
easy eyes inhaling the immobility of time.

Though these selected embodiments of secret gatherings instill a stoic, poignant mystery; it's that mystery which challenges the yearning mind.

I ambiance

I am the beginning of that who I am.
I am the earth and the sun and the stars.
I am the seed and the flower of faith.
I am the life and the living.
I am the way and the path.
I am the growth and the growth within.
I am the winds of the sky and the sea.
I am the circle in the cycle of life.
I am the rock and its sculptor.
I am the oak and my shelter is benevolent.
I am the innocence and the essence of love.
I am the learning and the teaching.
I am the knowing in all that there is and is not.
I am the light and the glow is my comfort.
I am the energy, the originator and receptor.
I am the soul and to soar is my resurrection.
I am the presence and it is here that I am.
I am the now and the future forever.
I am the infinity for eternal I am.

Back Soon

blank eyes
bleak disguise
wise eyes seek
wide eyes peek
nothing nighs
frustration flies
. . . to time beyond time fleeting by

empty find
stymied mind
mindless words
flightless birds
no thoughts
forget me naughts
. . . on the edges of rivers bone dry

* * * *

    Overbearing cadence herald the paradigms of his present existence; for he entered into this life as a Quixote out of Chaos.

Knightfall

Through the rhythm of the night he came,
    across the howling, growling seas;
    riding through the terror trees.
The Knight, Sir Dire; crouched astride
    his swift and sturdy steed, Blackfire.

    (continues)

Prodding through murk and plodding through mire
    seeking the ire of dragons spouting grim desire.
Thru the rhythm of the night he rode from fear
With sinewy arm outstretched;
    clenching his blood encrusted spear
A tom-tom's beat, the stallion's feet
    go pounding out of sight
    pounding, pounding, pounding thru the night
Nostrils flaring, black eyes glaring;
    in frenzy, Blackfire strode
Astride his back of sweaty black,
    Sir Dire, in utter anger rode
Sir Dire, his hazy, glazing,
    blazing, determined eyes afire
Sought the dragons; the searing,
    sneering dragons of the night
Escaping from the looming blooming dawn
He never saw, no he never saw
    the early morning light
Sir Dire still rides his steed, Blackfire
    amid the echoes and the rhythms of the dark
Forever seeking that elusive dragon;
His bloody useless spear,
    will never, oh no never find its mark
Hooves so fleet, the stallions feet
    go pounding out of sight
        pounding, pounding, pounding thru the night

The Leaving

Walking away from an accustomed life,
    from a space of lifetime belonging
Walking away
    all the symbols detaching
      all the signs yielding
        all the faces
          all the places
            dim and diffuse into a haze
And I muse and gaze upon
      a blank picture screen
         in some dark, remote, alien theater

Here and There

here in the valley
here in the dell
here in this haven
here I do dwell
      gone from the valley
      gone from the dell
      gone from the haven
      gone from the shell
there in the valley
there in the dell
there in that haven
there I did dwell

I am but one man walking the land
roots torn asunder, in a new place I stand.

The Prince of Light

an enchanted concept   coming from the outer fars
skipping o'er the sun   step-stoning the stars
a wispy spirit imagery   an emancipated soul
like a dawning mist   spreading tho'ts of gold
happiness his banner   love crested on his vest
sowing wisdom seeds   true peace his final quest
prince of light   his truth a keen honed knife
rending fear and greed   resurrecting life

A Fawn . . . . A Child

nestled in a hoar hound shallow
beyond a stalwart   hickory tree
bogged in mire,   left to fallow
bleating fawn lay in woeful misery

oh, some high and mighty hunter
gunshot scattered   o'er the land
firing at the slightest little quiver
power pumping in his trigger hand

huddled in a bombed-out hollow
behind a snare   of steel debris
bogged in fear   dust a swallow
bleeding child lies in wide-eyed agony

now the big guns   cry in terror
hatred festered   heinous dreams
to stop   a sinister omen bearer
a hand of justice wields and schemes

Good Goose Rhymes

1
Diddle, doodle, dumpster, dump
Mind in slumber, stagnant slump
Give a shove. a knock, a bump
Get up, get out, get off your rump

2
drifters in the wind are riders
sliding thermals, buoyant striders
going along on borrowed time

be the force, the wind, the driver
wielding blade, an artful carver
headstrong in creative mime

3
rainforests spring from fertile ground
foot loose and fancy free
ideas create constructive thoughts
imagination is the key

4
diddle, daddle, dumbwit, kumquat spittle
took refuge in numbers so hid in the middle
got lost in the crowd so here comes the riddle
in a manner of speaking too much is too little

Lepidoptera Magic

he flits from time to time
seemingly going nowhere
yet somehow with purpose
resting now and then
        pacific, in repose
letting his fans
    flex slowly in the sun

but it's the flight
        the soft flight
delicate bobs
    in determined thrusts
        frantic hues glistening
   nervous blurs scampering

then, in kind, they meet
     encircling, cavorting
      twisting about, turning
     kissing, pirouetting

gentle tinker bells
    monarchs of the sky
    dancing butterflies

Easy Come, Easy Go

he sought and wrought
on golden dreams he pondered
on silken trails he wandered
the thoughts he caught
were brought to naught
lottery winnings squandered

Trails

Walking and talking with God is a conversation in prayer. A stroll through and among his miraculous handiworks inspires anyone to glorify His existence. Admitting Him into your own being lets you see the world through His eyes. Trails to nowhere now become entrances to total understanding of Him being present in your thoughts.

... of the forest, of the meadows,
    of the skies, of the seas
... of the fishes, of the birds,
    of the grasses, of the trees
... of the gardens of His world
    the seeds of life He sows
... in the gardens of our world
    the blooms of love He grows
... thru His hand and His heart
    He has sculptured the way
... thru His love and His comfort
    I need not ever go astray

Gabriel's Windsong

Here and there, there and here
Everywhere; yet, nowhere near

Deeply shadowed by a splintery crippled ladder
a rusty un-honed sickle spears a dust encrusted horn

Wailing dormant silence from its brassy bladder
there upon a misty morning in a musty barn so worn

A wandering lad, strolling from some forgotten land
a haven bed to lay and soothe his aching tired feet

The musty barn beckoned to his yearning heart's
command; he dreamt amid lofty hay and shafted wheat

No place on this earth he would ever learn to favor
he dreamt of vagabonds, minstrels and servants free

To have his own toy that he might fondly savor
he dreamt his single simple wish would come to be

(continues)

Just before the dawning and with all the yawning
tweaking shadows of the mist were whisked and
forced to hide

Barn beams creaked and squeaked, squealing,
shrieking the horn shook and slipped away from the
sickle's side

As if through some eerie calling, the trumpet began
falling; landing so ever softly by the dreamer's cradled
eyes

Startled, quickly waking, the boy, abandonment
forsaking; brazen brass embraced in his arms and
joyous cries

As a fish is to his ocean
    or a love transcends emotion
The fingers and the trumpet played in perfect unison
The winds of time and motion
    bore seeds of his devotion
Now soul angels dance within the hearts of everyone

Here and there, there and here
Everywhere; yet, nowhere near

Rodin on the Shelf

he sits there all day long
pondering
contemplating the weight of his world
weighing his thoughts
waiting effortlessly for answers that may never be
what is heavy on his mind?
what of his world?
thinking has become his burden
what is mine?
what is yours?
what is ours?

Degrees of the Heart

alone, shivering, shedding icicle tears
    frozen stares splintering a vulnerable heart
Cold.

alone, emotionless, aloof, standing apart
    shadowed eyes masking the calculating heart
Cool.

alone, sensuous, seven torrid veils slithering
    tempting eyes taking hope from a lonely heart
Hot.

together, cuddling, sharing sun-swept smiles
    tender eyes offering love from a giving heart

Warm.

Burnout

decaying petals off the rose
    dying embers on the vine
gone is the delightful taste
    for the honey and the wine

Re-entry

rekindle your fire of life
    flaring strong, blazing new
burn another candle bright
    a unique tack, a novel view

The Waiting Game

frustration stalks
the streets of his id
    yet the poet keeps searching for rhyme
elusive words skirt the edge of his muse
    just as a dream with the passage of time
some omen to seek
some symbol to find
some thing to offer a clue
some finger to tickle his intellect
    just as the dawn glow tickles the dew

Proof Positive Times Four

1
dashing up the downstairs
getting nowhere fast
gerbil on a treadmill
tomorrow in the past
seek a lane of freedom
find the plane to ever-last

2
wherever you go, whatever you do
keep all your wits together
forever in time, endeavor to climb
smiles brighten up the heather

3
those who seek will aptly find
those things that seem elusive
roadblocks in an unlocked mind
    are really not obtrusive

4
stay not as a fetus cocoon curled
push out and find another world

. . . The Beginning . . .
On, On, Moving On

Chapter Eleven:

On, On, Moving On

Preface

You know, I love the eagle; so majestic, flying high and soaring in an even more majestic way.

Yes, I love the eagle; so regal, a symbol representing this great country of ours.

I love the eagle; so represented as a reward and a reminder of my youth.

I love the eagle; so magnificent a bird among all birds.

But have you noticed, or even having noticed, wondered why he is always peering downward? Yes, he's looking for prey, searching for his next meal for himself or for his eaglets. Understandably, his searching for prey is a matter of survival. However, by human standards and values, that is not an admirable attribute.

In order for any one of us to move on, we must look up, - forward and up. We should search for possibilities everywhere while aspiring upward. We should not prey on others to achieve those possibilities. However, in order to attain those seemingly impossible goals, we should seek help. Your help comes from God and those around Him and from within your soul through your own beliefs and faith. You revere your faith that your God and his friends are there to help you and your faith that your goal is an attainable possibility.

This, my eleventh book, is a Moving On. On and On, forward and upward.

Emergence

When the paws of coiling waters crush
    the pools of idyllic dreams
    and the claws of roiling slaughters hush
    the ghouls of pathetic screams

Then, and only then,
    will any rhyme claim reason
    or for any reason, - rhyme

And when all creative words conceived
    send sounds to a gifted hand
    that hand that takes that gift received
    to sow the shifting barren sand
    is that hand that instills creative growth
    in the minds and hearts of his fellow man

So move on and out and let it be
    let the winds and stars run free
    let the mind dwell in spontaneity
    let the heart speak with joviality
    yet retain a sense of humility
    loving and living compassionately
    believing in each other relentlessly
    forever and ever eternally
Let it be

The Plight of the Bumbling Pea

Skip P. Nutbutter -   the sociopath legume freak
    who feeds on unsuspecting veggie fems
    was caught stalking Cella Ree last week
Within her crisp, yet juicy, curving stems
    he truly and passionately yearned to spread
    but was debased and brusquely smeared instead
    between two lifeless slabs of jellied bread
Sentence served and justice dealt
Yet Cella Ree - so lithe and svelte
Still stalks the aisles of the grocery belt
    While taunting the eyes of every veggie freak

As to the pitiful plight of the bumbling pea
Destined to confinement in a jar as you see
On the shelves with the jelly and the jam; all three
Remains the odds-on pick of the foods each week

Sucking Our Freedom Away (SOFA)

Lawyers legislating laws
Our own lethargy
Sofa bound destiny
Don't pray
Don't walk
Don't talk
Don't say
    What's on your mind today
Don't stand up for your belief

Can't move - no sale
    Nice house but now our jail
Advertise, but don't discriminate
    "serene living" is against children
    "professional" is elitist
       as is "private" and "unique"
Be careful what you say and do
Big brother is out there watching you

SOFA FOR SALE
    Here come the takers
Going
Going
Gone

Only Yesterday

Just only yesterday
when I used to play
and hide and seek
and dream and speak
of all neat things
like having wings
to fly to Mars
or slide between the stars
or climb moonbeams
now all that seems
like only yesterday
but that's okay
for by then my four sons
and I had all the funs
as we laughed and played
my youth returned and stayed
within me and I smiled
I'd found again my inner child
yet days marched on
and soon their youth had gone
I searched but not in vain
for all that I did gain
was within my heart and soon
whistling a remembered tune
I skipped upon my merry way
as if only yesterday
now my golden child is near
and only yesterday is here

Seeing the Bud in a New Light

Picking up the teardrops fallen
    from the petals of despair
Nature's fondly savored pollen
    urge the blossom to declare
That the thorns along its branches
    are not omens to beware
Alight along the face that blanches
    joy and happiness is there

Foxfire

Shadows falling and the trees are calling me
    to the dense forest in my burning soul
    tho'ts are evergreen and yearning
    the glow within a deep discerning
    far better than a dark forbidding hole

I know there is a light tho' faintly glowing
    a light that is steadfastly in control
    to keep that light within - a beacon
    then I - the keeper; yea the deacon
    will maintain life's focus and a goal

like being mired in a rain forest
yet seeing not a single tree
one must remember that the sun is still alive
and there is music everywhere

when creative juices flow

so easy to say
      yet harder to do
         a dichotomy of life
between the words and the you

just how many poets
      or wise men of grace
         dwell on morose and chagrin
but speak of heavenly space

through the hope of the many
    or the wisdom of a few
      life's transformations
prance from the old to the new

The Question

'tis the same age old question
of just why we are here
did we evolve from some being,
or in His image, just appear?
where did I come from?
where will I go?
where lies the answer,
if found - will I know?
each self is a mystery
a conundrum enshrined
each soul is so tenuous
rapt in a cavernous mind
what propels me to seek
is that something akin
compels to find
that something within
a new mood-scape is painted
by a symphonious breeze
as I dance with the flowers
and converse with the trees
could this be the answer
to the question I ponder,
that this earthly commune
is the gate to the yonder?
but is there a yonder
to which – in faith - I aspire?
if there is more beyond faith
then what quests my desire?

The Touch

though the fingers tap the music
the words flow forth in measured time
through the impulse of an instant
memories explode in treasured rhyme
      touch the keyboard oh so slightly
      the words appear oh so sprightly
  miracles delighting
  automatic writing
  messages descending
  oracles portending
      grab your standard, bear it tightly
      streak thru time, show it brightly
all the shamans; all those who care
are the souls in this sphere you share

etchings on a leaf
    nature's wounds unscarred in time
        yet the burden's forever carried
cruel caresses breed wild beauty
        unfettered by judgmental jargon
imagination taken beyond infinity
        beauty beyond any artist's dream
spontaneous etchings scribbled
        by the hands of a masterful mind
a kaleidoscopic universe revealed
        as etchings come and etchings go
lighthouse beams revolve in comfort
        yet permanency spurts and passes
though time is etched upon this leaf
        this leaf, though brief, moves on

The Cicada Brief

It wasn't the cause that captured my inquisitive eye,
But the frantic motion of one single Baltic Ivy leaf.

Emerging slowly from the earth, one August morn,
I spied a mud-encrusted shell traversing an ivy stem –
As an old man awakening stiff from a big deep sleep.

Plodding across a rustic railroad tie, instinctively;
only to disappear again in the verdant forest of ivy.

Tonight I might hear him drone on in a shrill staccato;
or maybe spy his exo-bones, the sentinel to his past;
clutching the spruce bark in an eerie eternal climb.

We sometimes hear what we never see; then marvel
When we have the chance to see and hear. Marvel then
turns into wonder and awe for this humble experience.

Miracles, so gigantic, yet so minute, are within us all!

Though he's a loose goose
    or sometimes obtuse.
You must admit that Dr, Suess
Sets your sluice to flow
    with creative juice…..

Suess Land
Mired in "tock-sick" waste

Find the sox
Next to the rox
Under the fox
Who's munching the phlox
From behind the box
Just below the clox
With their noisy tick-tox

The Outlook

set your sights and set your ways
    on heavenly nights and heavenly days
for there are times when nothing rhymes
    and troubled lives when nothing thrives
but faith that keeps and love that heaps
    will bring a smile that lasts a while.

May I tell you a story that may not make sense
yet may harbor beginnings of great consequence.
An epic of wonder that I do truly believe
will only bear pains to the hapless naïve.

Rise and Shine

A galactic explosion, blowing seeds on a cosmic foray;
planting timeless scions o'er the firmament's display.
What harbinger contents would these casings contain?
What ominous portents would their presence explain?
No regional bias, - no comfy nestling space –
instantaneous touch pioneering endearing embrace.
Growth lay in patience; eyes discerning no change,
an object so shapeless remained ever so strange.
Telepathic messages emitting from a well, deep within,
sprinkled with a plea piercing, - minds swirling in spin.

"lift my wings and fly me higher and higher
let me soar, slide and glide, ne'er to tire
higher! higher!
as the fingertips of a roaring fire
lift me! lift me!
higher than the highest cathedral spire
higher than the sky and higher!
free me from these bonds so dire
let me go! Oh, let me go!
lift me higher!   HIGHER!"

(continues)

spying nary a handle, no lever; without any door
perhaps here before me stands a mammoth metaphor
my plea said to "lift"; and, in vain, so I did try.
even mountains may be moved if the right tools I apply
as a hanging fog arises in an early dawning sun
so too the task of releasing this grand phenomenon
pools of innocence rippled to precipitous ledges
joyously cascading to the realms of realistic edges
a sense of understanding permeated thru my being
a dream became a feeling and believing became seeing

"we are exploding stars, - novae,
we are stardust on a rebirth high
cosmic sliders, riders of the sky
we live - we die
our dust does fly! does fly!
to dream, to learn, to know,
to land, to sow, and then to grow.
until the burning urge to lift and go –
and once again to fly! to fly!
higher! higher! beyond the newborn sky!

Venues

Do I wake or do I sleep?
Do I laugh or do I weep?

If there is no cut; - then why the lesion?
Is there a rhyme without good reason?

Who stalks these lanes which lead to nowhere?
What gives with the sound of one hand clapping;
   or a crash of feathers in the breezes flapping?

As I sleep, great dreams are lost – forsaken.
Yet those remembered spark the best path taken!

Hold That Thought

There is no thought if it never leaves the thinker.

******

He who dwells in the house of self
is but a dusty book up on the shelf.

******

Open the book and let it be read;
just as you think, so let it be said.

Exit Right

Every day is just like any other
Day in, day out, totally redundant
Old stagnant thoughts abundant
Approach the same old door
- revolving

Each new day brings a new tho't
With each new tho't, a new idea
With each idea, a new approach
With each approach, a new door
- evolving

Playwright

dream weaver of thoughts, of words, of schemes
    having reached this stage of his life play,
fingers having yet to shake hands with his mind
    a cocooned audience sits in stoic silence
he frustrates in his ineptness to perform
    as one unkind scene cascades upon another

how does he refocus……..re-establish his role
return to a oneness………..with his yearning soul

his haunting players…….portray a dismal cast
lines of rote…………………..from the scenery of his past

he must move onward….he must take the lead
reweave his dreams……..from his inherent seed

taking a cue from his ever-present Prompter
    he casts aside the demon threads from hell
reweaving reborn dreams into living themes
    his play emerges as do his butterflies
flapping a glorious din of gratitude
    their long awaited freedom now reprieved

Who Cares?

Rising, setting, spectrum blending, warmth extending,
    another day – who cares?
Blossoms bursting, branches bearing, love-wings
    singing, another spring – who cares?
Been there, done it, seen it, won it,
    wrote another ho-hum sonnet – who cares?
Tempers flaring, el-nino scaring, warlords daring,
    another fear – who cares?
Parents sighing, offspring crying, growing, leaving,
    another life – who cares?

Precious gems among the stones,
    drenched in brilliant tones.
Shining stars sparkling bright,
    even during the blackest night.
Each life a gem – and then a star,
    romancing hope – greetings from afar.
Who cares?
    I care, I care, I care!

Daffodils in Freeze

In the winter stillness
A brrrrrrr is in the air
Bare branches thrash in frenzied waves
The March lion cries out with icy roars
Angry clouds sneer at the cowering sun
Yet yellow buds burst from the dormant beds
So eager to say: *"Hello, dear year!"*
So eager to bring well-wishing cheer
Cold yellow iced over – brittle to the gentle touch
Daffodils shivering in a bed of rainbows
Spring isn't ready – ole man winter roars too much
Hold the cold. Stay the day.
Let the hue change the soul from harsh to tender
And settle there to remain in dazzling splendor

Alone in Silence

Amidst a forest wayside – beneath a tempting tree
Sitting in a tranquil trance – be still; so much to see

Alone in silence
   In the wilderness
      Breathless
      Listening
      Waiting
   In the hush
   Wilderness speaks
   "The Earth is at peace."
Silence is golden.

Moon's Caper

At the still during the night
    Shapes labored in whisper
Moonshines all around them
    The cache is their silver

In the still of the night
    And the earth is a whisper
Moonshine's all around me
    Shapes dressed up in silver

Fancies

figure me this; fancy me that
what in the world are you looking at?
    lacy lamps, vivacious vamps,
    skinny scamps, chortling champs,
    tattered tramps, or images of your soul
    in the kaleidoscope of your fantasies.
how unreal is your reality?
how real is your fantasy?
do you know where you are going, or even know
    where you are coming from?
walking across the quicksand
    into the jungle of unknown fears,
drenched by the downpour of omnipresent tears
holding on to the sturdy roots of life
sneering at the demon who wields his brazen knife
move on, undaunted; follow your fancies, move on.

The Last Supper

the alien peered down
on our alien land,
so famished
his power was all too grand,
yet, he hungered
the world was his oyster,
our alien land held in his alien hand.
one bite, one gulp, and it was gone.
yummy, so tasty, so grand.

Rockwell-an Americana

Croquet –
    high on the edge of a river overlook
    on a Sunday summer sunny afternoon.
Long flowing dresses hiding tender skin.
Blacks and whites were playing not a racial game.
And, nearby,
    under the titillating shade of an old oak tree,
    sitting and rocking in a circle, -
        bonnets chattering, talking,
        beards nodding, listening,
        all laughing, participating,
        in a little black boy's birthday.
Happy talk, happy day, - picture perfect.
Witnessed, yet captured only in my mind.
Now gone, but ne'er forgotten.

Dream Flight

Tranquil beds holding tiny tousled heads
    murmuring screams of frazzled fright
Hearts are pounding mightily
    in the dreary dark and lonesome night

Tranquil beds holding tiny tousled heads
    peeking towards the slowly closing doors
Soon sleepy souls spin heroic roles
    o'er kaleidoscopic distant fabled shores

Flushing tender dreams of splendor
    to relish in dazzling demeanors of delight
Complete just as the dreary dark is broken
    by the wayward wings of early morning light

The dawn of forgotten dreams may portend
    the consciousness of a clear and present time
Yet, these tousled heads begin again, instead,
    to play their roles of innocence sublime

Hello! Who's there?

What, pray tell, are all the pleasures of your heart?
    Do you think, "All's well."
        And you've nothing to impart?

Is your life that bleak or your body just too weak?
    Does your soul want to go out of your mind,-
        So to speak?

Are the milky moon, the sparkly stars, the soothing sun
    oblivious to your dreams of being with all is one?

Are the festooned webs of silvery threads
    in your tethered mind
        weaving a cocoon of tattered shreds,
            yourself, now hard to find?

Turn and face the door of golden life,
    and open up your heart.
        Go on up the down staircase.
            Please try and do your part.

Sorry, this lion is busy

There once was a lion who sulked in his pride
Living only for himself, all kindred aside
His muse was his cloak
His bane was his yoke
Solitude harbored hidden hatred inside

Fleeting Melancholia

Pheasants in fright
    Flushed into flight
    Leaving a hush in the emerging dawn
        Vibrant thoughts all but stolen away

What escapes now, leaving the blank empty mind
    With no wonders to favor
    Nor revelations to savor
        Ideas non-existent in the budding light

Smell the wonders of the rose
    Smell the rose; scent dies; scent goes
    Remembrance wanes, the rose,
        The scent, goodbye, - so long

Campfire sparks prance heavenward
    Dashing and slashing, disappearing in a flash,
    Fireflies dancing in staccato light
        Pin-sprinkling the stillness of the night

All now right here. Not there. Now gone. Nowhere.
    Nowhere to be found.
    Lost in the scheme of things.
        Fleeing on cobwebbed cocooned wings

Putting a Stop to the Blues

Live for the moment.
Seek, accept and believe in the truth.
Enter in to the life of my Living God.
Let Jesus Christ take control of my soul.
Welcome Him. Savor Him. Relish in His Glory.
Accept His Benevolent Presence.
Believe. Surrender. Embrace. Glorify. Celebrate.
Open His Gift of Love and Forgiveness.
Be thrilled in the Glow of His Empowered Light.
Explore my soul and discover Life through Him.
Let the rivers of hope flow through my total being.
Let the big bang of His Holy Universe
Explode within me.

Let All be One.
Honor one and all.
Love is divine.
Let my will become His Will.
Venture into my new world
with a new heart and a new beginning.
Walk with confidence, humility and reverence.
My love is the foundation that faith is built upon.
The strength of my Lord sustains me.
Life is beautiful.
All is well.
All is One.

Delta Force

Three corners meet, touch, greet one another
    as a timeless point, approaches, retreats
    to the sanctum of a somewhere space,
        a somewhere place.
Face to face with my continuum being,
    I see myself looking out, looking in:
    yet enclosed, encased, alone in space.
Boggled images flash, dash, crash through
    crazy cobwebbed corners, split asunder;
    sent to new highs,
        new ideas, new beginnings.
I careen through meadows of dreams,
     through waves of wonderment,
     through caresses of tingling crystals of snow,
     through rising, soaring,
        enveloping forest cathedrals.
The joyous heart aches in blissful awe.
I want.
I need.
And, in a frenzy,
I feed on the thoughts I breed.
And I am freed to seed,
    to blossom in the dawn and dew.
All focused.
All fresh.
All new.

Godspeed.

Dancing with Clouds

Ultra soft
   touching
      feathers in the wind
         darting
            playing
               dancing
         grasping at nothing - feeling all.
As eagles soar, so do I,
   higher and higher,
      swooping
         looping
            gliding
               sliding
                  enveloping
             enshrouding
dancing with clouds.
Enraptured and captured,
   His buoyancy strengthens me,
      uplifting my soul
         unburdening my heart.
Through His gentleness,
   His softness,
         His joy,
            His warmth,
               His love,
I hide, glide and ride.
      I abide and confide in His grandeur,
           enthralled, I go on.

Whither Samaritans, do ye go

why all the worldly wizards allow all the languid
    lizards to wriggle and squiggle through
      the blizzards, dwelling in all their empty souls?

an undernourished mother bleakly lying, dying
    in the dusty, crusty dirt. A likewise child,
    pleading eyes wild, parched lips agape,
    silently crying hurt.

a malcontented miser, wallows in a whirlpool
    of delirious obsessions, sneering and
      snickering; counts and recounts
        all of his possessions.

whither all the good Samaritans who wander to and fro?
whither do they go?

These next three poems are written about the game of croquet.

Court Sense

Be it friend or be it foe
Be it gentleman or dame
Be it young or be it old
Croquet is the name of the game.

We've played the strategic game of chess
We know the angled shots of pool
We all can putt pretty well, I guess
So, if you please, all of these help to
      Make us croquet cool

Neither creaking back nor rusting frame
Will squelch this hobbled bloke
We love this fun, though humbling game
We'll play until the day we croak

It certainly is a wicket game to play
And it is a game for roques
It is a cunning deft display
Stroked by proper white cloaked folks

Some Cheap Shots

God, it's such a big bright ball;
I can't believe I stroked and missed it!
No hocus pocus,
        All you need to do is focus.

With all these rules, it's hard to lick it.
'Just take your clip to your bloody wicket!'
No hocus pocus,
        All you need to do is focus.

He who keeps his head in gear
Has a better chance to wicket clear.
No hocus pocus,
        All you need to do is focus.

Stroke that ball and follow through
to the target straight and true.
No hocus pocus,
        All you need to do is focus.

Something wicket this way comes

Over the dunes each surged and poured
Wielding a wooden mallet sword
    White specters in their frenzied thrill
    Determined to ply their sporting skill
    By stalking each foe in an earnest will
They sought to vanquish this croquet lord

Taking his turn, the duels began
A scheming break, the balls he ran
    Shots of glory. Thoughts do endear
    Frustration grows as frowns appear
    Wicket ten he stroked through clear
Would no one stop this wicket man?

Sideline patience, she calmly waited
His fault, her turn, with confidence she stated
    "I am the master of my fate.
    I call the shots, make no mistake;
    I'll rush and pass him to the stake.
Ta-Ta, Wicket Man, your ego's been deflated."

A Sense of Purpose

When in the process of finding yourself
    Search all the rooms and all the realms
        Of your whims and of your dreams
        Of your deeds and of your schemes
    Search all the corners and all the niches
        Of your thoughts so enigmatically hidden
        Of your desires so lecherously forbidden

When in the process of finding yourself
    Search thoroughly the labyrinth of your heart
        Where your feelings instilled, do dwell
        Where your misgivings mired, do swell
    Search within the complex sanctum of your mind
        In all the nooks and crannies of your id
        In the memories of all you said and did

When in the process of finding yourself
    Search beyond your mind and heart and selfish spaces
        Into the lofty Kingdom of the Lord above
        Into His all endearing and forgiving Love
    Search your soul to reason for the purpose of your living
        Accept your God, thru faith, justifies your being
        Accept his Love, and thru Him, you will be seeing

Ponder

Pondering all the wonder exploding within like thunder, I relish and embellish all the whims that I may plunder from the cache contained here inside my heart and soul.

If any thought cannot be caught, then I am but a 'muser'. For then the wonder is but a blunder; truly, I'm a loser. The cache is; there is no cache, but just a mighty hole.

The truth I face in this place and in this time sublime. Is the knowledge gained has not restrained this rhyme, so I can truly claim my cache as part of my heartfelt goal.

Dewdrop Tinctures

Just a tiny drop of hope is all you need
For a tiny drop of faith to hold on to the hope
Just a tiny drop of love to hold on to the faith
Three small drops hold the miracles of life
Or
Hope is the dew at dawn
Faith is the bloom
Love is the life
Miracles abound
All around
All is found
All is one

When Dreams Become You
Life's whetstone, keened and preened
Where sharper images emerge
Honed by a cutting edge
Where alluring themes
Become enduring dreams; - so it seems
I step through the looking glass and I become me – free
No longer a mere reflection of my illusionary peers
Nor a recollection of any of my suspecting fears
I stand, sharp and ready for the coming day.
And what a day it is! There is no daily grind
The sun is bright   The sky is blue
I am as high as a kite
The day is sharp. My attitude is clear and at its height
Seizing the moment, I savor all my erstwhile memories

Sometimes
Sometimes
I wonder where this day will take me
Then I wander and sit and ponder over yonder
Growing fonder of the day and who I'm going to be
Sometimes
Nature plays games of 'hide and seek' with me
All the critters sneak warily about and peer in doubt
Eyeing, creeping slowly nearer, with utmost curiosity
Sometimes
No ideas stop and linger for a while with me
It is, as if, I'm staring at a world; so dank and silent
Filling my tearful eyes and hopeful sighs; - nil to see
But most times
The day is bright and gay and full of glee
For I see all the things that give me joy and happiness
Endearing me to relish all the love so enveloping me

Something about Nothing

Once in a time of nowhere there dwelt a gnome of great renown. He had supreme domain over nothing in nowhere; yet everything belonged to him as long as he reigned supreme. The logic of nowhere was that everything was not as it would seem and if it seemed logical, it probably wasn't.

He was known everywhere as Syllabus; - Syl for short. Even though he was tall of stature; he had his shortcomings. Syl spent most days busily doing everything for nothing. He would harm no one and could do no evil. Matter of fact, Syl was good for nothing. Every morning, at first light, he would dry the dusty dew from his golden toadstool throne in the boonie-bogs of nowhere. Then he would sit there and muse the remainder of his nowhere near perfect day. No one came to see him, laud him, taunt him or sit in awe of him. Everything and everyone was nowhere to be found.

He was relentless in his belief that everyone was below him and they, obviously, were from nowhere.

Syl, in order to create some modicum of order, established his profound Memorandum of Understanding; which he carved into the trunk of the eucalyptus tree precariously growing on the very edge of an abyss overlooking nowhere. In order for anyone to read the essence of his profoundness, the reader had to dangle precariously from the already precariously dangling eucalyptus tree. Neither has anyone read it, nor have they lived while trying to read it. To this very day, no one understands anything and everything is bogged down somewhere in nowhere.

    Syllabus reigns supreme. The epitome of the abstract and decider for all. Second to none, Syl remains a sycophant toadstool warmer. He levies wrath on all evil doers and nay-sayers; as well as those who never came before him nor will ever come after him.

From This Time Forward

From this time forward, go stroll amongst the flowers
    and caress the splendor,
        smell the essence and reflect therein.

Go to the very edge of the still waters, stoop; and let
    your fingertips instill ripples,
        sending echoes to the far reaches.

Perk up and listen to the silence of amazement which is
    around you; abounds you,
        astounds you, envelops you.

Let your body feel the tingling of excitement
    of just being; feeling the pleasures of your
        wonderful world here within.

(continues)

Go to the forest and marvel amidst its majestic
    verdant awe, seek the hidden wizardry
        of its creativities and mysteries.

Embrace the soul of a tree and peer into its stark
    roughness. Explore the patterns of a structured,
        yet delicate fern meadow.

With each footfall trod upon the soft touch of a moss
    carpet. Breathe in and savor
        every aromatic nuance given to you.

Reach to the soil and, in your hand, lift
    and sift its pleasure; its warmth;
        its coolness; its life; its dreams; its comfort.

Lift your eyes to the treetops, so high above;
    and gaze and trace the lacy patchwork,
        the hallmark of the Master Painter.

Lift your eyes higher and let them dance
    in the cotton fluff. Let your imagination
        carry you to the reaches of your desires.

Do all of this in solitude. Be alone with your soul.
    Relish the moment and you will
        be refreshed from this time forward.

Whose hands are these?

Whose hands are these?
    Reaching out to touch me, hold me, thrill me.
    Graceful limbs entwining every fiber of my
        being
    Could there ever be another time so winsome,
        so entrancing, so enhancing,
        so akin to my yearning soul?
Whose hands are these?
        meeting, grasping, greeting?
Whose hands are these?
        in this place, this time, this rhyme?
Who stays my thoughts and holds them in silent favor?
All these longings and belongings in cherished savor;-
        who is this unselfish loving soul?
I can never cease to stroll in wonder.
I can forever seek to dwell within the aura of his soul.
For those warm and gentle hands will guide me home.

All that I have

All that I have is yours
All that you have given me is also yours
The bond of life is the love that we share
The faith that dwells within enlightens and strengthens
And the love of life is consumed by the abounding joy

I am daily refreshed by your presence
I remain awestruck with your earthly handiwork
But I remain reticent to express my feelings to mankind

If the love, and the faith, and the life is to be here now
with my fellow man as it is to be with you; then give
me the strength to express that joy to the world.

Who

Who Is
Who Is the One
Who Is The One Who is?
Are You the One?

I stand in the shadows at the very edge of my id
And I marvel at all of the mighty things you did
As I enter into your light of total understanding
I emerge into a serene sense of love, gently landing

No one can express the feelings of their being
One can not believe the thoughts I'm now retrieving
There is a wrenching, burning, yearning in my soul
There is a mystic aura of becoming a part of the whole

Even the darkest shadows of demons screeching fright
Nor the cries of pleading minions fading from my sight
May deter me from escaping this determined task
Give me your fervent guidance, Lord; that is all I ask.

You
You Are
You Are The One
You Are The One Who Is

The following two entries were written upon our return from Germany. My wife, Shirley, and I celebrated our fiftieth wedding anniversary at the residence of our nephew, Eric. He was the Consul General of Bavaria and we were in Munich. What a great time that was!

Prelude to a Munich Fest

Achtung!

The essence of an effervescence pleasure is the preponderance of frothy bits of bubbles dancing about one's bulbous nose as one imbibes the beverage of one's pleasure.

Suffice to say that no vices are involved and no extemporaneous devices are deployed.

The perpetrated imbiber revels in the sole anticipation of the quaff set before his steadfast eyes and the eventual rise of the overflowing amber stein approaching his already greedy grinning lips.

The first gulp is gigantic and orgasmic, but far from climactic. He relishes in the gluttonous pleasures of his simple desires. He wallows in extreme ecstasy as he swallows the nectar of brewery gods. Further suffice that no man can ever revisit this event again with the same fervor.
    Prosit! Gemeutlichkeit!
    Auf Wiedersehen.

Majestic Enrapture Capture

A tranquil mist rises o'er the lea
    Feathers stir in frenzied flight
As an eager omen bearer stalks
    The stillness just as he might
Crickets' cackle ceases
    Antlers stare in a patient anticipated hold
Stoic forest sentinels wait until
    Something ominous is foretold

No man bears witness to
    Wondrous marvels of its mighty call
No man holds any audience
    With all creatures large and small
One may only imagine how it comes
    To be each and every morn
When the wilderness awakens
    As a new growing dawn is born

The fingers of this writer
    Have sprung to life this very day
Wondering, always wondering
    How far spaces dance and play
For each and every daybreak
    Brings the songs I now know so well
Like the Chuck Will's Widow
    Exercising his daily show and tell

For the first time in my life,
    I spent a week in Bavarian country air.
And I was witness to the sound   (continues)

Of song not common to my ear.
The ending of his plea sounded
    Like "stranger", so enamored me
Each morn in vain I searched
    For a bird I could not find nor see

And yet his seemingly 'unwelcome'
    Poignant cry, certainly to me,
Was as welcome and as beautiful
    As any overture could ever be
To find peace of mind in this war-torn
    Ravaged planet we call Earth
Is like finding hope and wisdom
    In all the good things of worth

I could sulk and wallow in all the greed
    And woe on any dire forsaken night
I could sit and worry that my
    Selfish skin was cringing in its plight.
Reality tells me in its wily way
    To be wary and yet seek the star
As it glistens on the canvas
    Of our heaven looking upon us from afar.

My world, as I hope is yours
    Is filled with musings such as these
Each day I revel in simple pleasures
    And my heart is put at ease
I bear no fear of any omen bearer
    Seeking danger to my body whole
The majesty of enraptured thoughts
    Has been captured here in my soul

Taking the Time to Rhyme

Queens and Kings, above all things;
    ruled the lowly pawns
What is more, Knights of yore, freed
    fair damsels in distress
And as time went by, the dragon's cry
    broke the fiery dawns
The epics told of adventures bold,
    in a time of deep duress
The scene was stark, the ages dark;
    all seemed woe-be-gones
But it's just a tale, and without fail;
    hope springs nonetheless

The mind ungluing, this rhyme pursuing;
    it is not an easy task
Yet once it's done, through toil and fun;
    'tis all that one can ask
Having taken the time to create the rhyme
    for a reader to pleasantly enjoy
I can only surmise is a blessing's disguise,
    for we poets to elegantly employ

Permutations and Lamentations

An absence of thought, especially in rhyme, totally eludes me from time to time. Poets experience the inspiration to create as an exasperating, frustrating specter peering from a clouded looking glass. It's there, but not graspable or discernable. Most times, an idea flourishes, a creation emerges from the deep dark recesses if the mind and a poem is consummated.

But not this time; -not today!

So, I pick myself up, grab the Windex and clean the mirror. All I get in return is a distinct, clearly discernable specter grinning back at me. In continued frustration, the Windex missile shatters the mirror and my thoughts are now just bits and pieces. Little snips of ditties and droll couplets are strewn about the cluttered disheveled room. A sharp mind would have caught this tirade in the throes of battle and prevented this mad dullard's handiwork from ever occurring.

So, with dust pan and broom in hand, the bits and pieces are swept up and tossed totally out of my mind. Sitting in placid morose, sans a grinning specter of doom, I remain utterly fascinated at how profound my vibrant creativity has shriveled. Something out of the box must re-ignite the spark within me.

So, I get up and gather the flint and floss in an attempt to create a spark to ignite the floss. As successful as I was; the big red sirens came and put out the remains of what was once this poet's exquisite lair.

(continues)

So, now I sit somewhere, bare, in a borrowed chair, with singed hair, a glazed stare, no care in the world, and still with a dare to write a poem with flair to share with my sweet 'au pair', so fair and debonair.

"Oh where, oh where has my little dog gone?
  Oh where, oh where can he be?"
  He went to the butcher to get a big bone
  He went with sweet 'au pair', but not me!

The Mystery of Myself

Uplifting, - berating, testing, constructing, exploring, discovering, - and ever wandering into the mysteries of myself.

About myself, to myself, from myself, of myself, unto myself, be myself, not myself, knowing myself, beyond myself. Behind myself, above myself, below myself, before myself, beside myself, within myself, without myself, for myself, against myself.

Me, myself and I, we ego three go dancing off into the night, ergo fancy free; - with giggling thoughts of ultra-glorious glee.

Life

Of The Boy
This apple in his hand, as you can see, was just plucked from the nearby apple tree. Now it's no longer part of the apple tree; just a fruit held in his hand, as you can see. Of all the apples in the tree, why he chose this one is a mystery.

Of The Apple
I feel elated, saddened, lonely, free, and naïve; knowing nothing of my destiny? Suddenly I ponder my purpose in this life, I am embarking on a new venture; having left my happy apple family. Yet, I feel confined and guided by a hand; and I'm sensing a feeling of captivity.

Espirit 'de Core'
I did not choose to join the Core. I was hand picked and now I am furious. And what's more, I feel I was deprived of my freedom of choice. I have no voice. I was elated that I was free when I left my family. I did feel lonely and maybe sad but I entered a new world. Why am I being held against my will? Where am I going?

Of The Boy
It was no mystery. He was happy he picked this apple for he thought he had picked the best one on the tree. At first, he thought he would eat it. Then he began to think of all the ways this apple could be utilized; - in a pie, a gift to somebody, a missile towards an enemy or just a juice in a jar. Lots of choices! Oh me! Which one will it be?

Of The Apple
Okay. I can not get up and walk away. I have resigned to my destiny. I am here to give to others; to sustain their livelihood. I am satisfied, and give myself freely. My seeds will somehow live on.

Of The Boy
He holds the apple in his hand and he is not hungry. He decides to give it away to someone who needs the apple more than he. He feels good about his choice. His day is fulfilled.

Of The Apple
Now I also am fulfilled.

Pie in the Sky

    This frantic old coot in a polka dot suit was pointing up to the sky! Look up! Look up!! With a pitiful cry, look up! Look up! <u>It's a pie!!!</u>
    Don't ask me why I said with a sigh. I'm just a guy who was just going by. What you have heard is absurd. It must be a bird,<u> not a pie</u>.!
    No-no, I know what I see, he swiftly told me. It's round and it's flat and it spins and all that. I'm scared. I'm too young to die. It's a pie!!
    It is not what it seems. You are having bad dreams. Why don't you just sit and rest for a bit. Then look up and see that there isn't a<u> pie</u>!
        (continues)

So he sullenly withdrew to a place that he knew and pondered his perplexing plight. He thought all night. "I know what's up in that sky!"

Now as you all know, this coot in a polka dot suit discovered this pie in the sky was really the baker who knew how to fly on high.
Chaos subsided and the populace divided into factions of doubt and deceit. I dare not repeat who went up to eat the pie in the sky
This tale is so old, and probably told many, many times over. But such are the dreams that show how happiness can give us a high
The polka dot coot jumped out of his suit and the fish ran away with the loon. The baker just up and died. The cow wondered why and the fork ran into the woods to spoon.

Hah!! I bet you thought all the time this was about a UFO. So little do you know.

Heaven Lea

A meadow explodes, blossoming into vibrant freedom
    swaying in a waving golden living awe
Sits there as an oasis, amid a vast largess of verdant
    trees, dark and standing so majestically tall

A gentle breeze entices tassel laden blades to ripple
    echoes across its amber broad expanse
One echo follows another and the lea begins to glow
    and flow, and prance and dance as in trance

All the creatures of the forest come to drink and savor
    the magic nectar in the haven of the lea
Prancing deer play Bambi games, while animals and
    birds and little things go hide and seek in glee

Nary any human being bares witness or sanctifies his
    soul to happier times like this
Yet he can very well imagine such a sight
    appreciating its exquisite bliss

How many such oases are playing scenes like this
    across our precious hallowed land?
How many are there that are, in turn, destroyed
    by man's needful and spiteful hand?

Alas! I, as a poet, cannot stop a war from far across
    our valued, cherished sea
But most certainly, I can cast a crusading plea
    for the eternal heaven lea

The Dawning

A moonbeam breaks into my sleepy room
Love blossoms begin to bloom
Diminishing the gloom
I love it! Oh, yes, how I love it
I do!
I do!
A speck of stardust strikes my wary eye
And my heart flutters with a sigh
I have a sudden yen to fly
I love it! Oh, yes, how I do love it
I do!
I do!
I do like the dark but wait for the light
Black back to bright
Breakfast delight
I love it! Oh, yes, how I love it
How true!
How true!
Now love is all around me in the air
And I need and want to care
And, above all to share
With you, my love, with you
I do!
I do!
In breaks the yawning dawn
And with it this song
To you, I belong
I do love you! Oh, yes, I do love you
I do!
I do!

A Poet's Task

To create a rhyme with sound design
The proper cache of thoughts defined
Are brought to pen if man might find
Those chosen words inside his mind

The Silhouette

Lonely tree   -   top lofty hill
Standing tall – standing still
Snugly lain   -   shadowed base
Serene dreamer – captured space

The Sentinel

Battered buoy - bashed by waves
Solo warning   -   toils and slaves
Clanging gong   -   thru the night
Wayward souls - welcome sight

Chalk Talk in a Blackboard Jungle
*(just some ins and outs of busy needles,
pointed remarks, stilted stitches, tattered
tales and sundry spins and yarns)*

1. Little Miss Muffed It

Once upon a pin cushion she did sit
Her nose in the air and she in a snit
No cares for the world – not one least bit
Her world is the stuff in her sewing kit

2. All Sewn Up

There was this big wheel from famed Karn
Who made tales weaving stitches and yarn
      He said midst his gin
     "These tales I will spin
As the big man; I just don't give a gosh darn"

3. Fork It

Sitting on a signpost at the fork of a winding road
A craven laden raven shrieked at a hopping horny toad
The right fork is the left one – mass destruction is
   forebode
If you stay the course – as I propose – bombs will
   explode

Hell's Afire

The mute flute and the thistle whistle sat amid the
    burning bush
Like a god the burning bush said to them, "there's no
    need to shush
"I will protect you from all evildoers running around
    this troubled land"
"Just go about your business. I am the maestro of this
    master grand."

The High and Mighty

Between dream schemes and brain drains;
    sits the mighty president
Thru all the turmoil and the folly
    no soul may dare dissent
When a mind in power in his tower
    believes he's heaven sent
No one ever saw it coming
    nor cares how the money's spent

Birds of a Feather

There is a maize craze in the wicked thicket
And the pleasant pheasant goes about his chores
There is a vulture culture brewing in the fallow hallow
Yet the dull gull only tends to his earthly mores

There is a darling starling soothing a sobbing robin
Both totally immersed in salving their own bones
Yet a tanager manager spins, swoons and wails
Mighty tales of wisdom to his awestruck crones

The Surge

Where have all our soldiers gone?
Who protects our rights - our song?
Dying embers on a once mighty fire
Hopes and dreams in smoke rise higher
Sons and daughters wield swords of pain
Striving to believe their plight is sane
Yet the surge goes on and on and on
More money and guns are forever drawn
Guardians waving our flag of the free
In what condition will our nation be?

Terror rages so America wages
An eternal costly escalating war
Youthful purge for troops to surge
Ever increasing more and more
We fear the fear of danger here
As we have never feared before
Just how long can we go on?
Is peace on sale at the corner store?

Our homeland is a borderline case
A "terrortory" of the United States
Schemes of wrath and dreams of gore
Now infiltrate our lands once more
Pillars of hatred on foundations rise
Truths spin out into outrageous lies
Slowly, slowly the black plague creeps
Across the plains and over the steeps
When will our nation open up its eyes?
Before we bade our town's goodbyes?

Chalk Talk Flip-Flop

Wow! Those last seven poems were reality, but so depressing that I would like to devote and would like to complete this eleventh book of poetry on a gentler and more serene tone. I have three poems left to write; perhaps a trilogy would be appropriate.

One: Glory Be!

Two: Willow

Three: We the People

One: Glory Be

Not the most beautiful flower
    But the lavender lovely delicacy is vibrant
Languishing amidst its pale tendril leaves
    Searching and stretching their way across the sand
The morning glory is a good wake-up call
      For all of us to see and ponder
To fully appreciate all the good upon our reverent land

Two: Willow

Misting dawn
    Beside a mirrored creek
Stands a hunching weeping tree
    A specter in serenity
Such a looming wonder seen on this silent morn

And, yet, there's more – a gentle breeze
    Long fingers reach and slowly breach
The stillness of the creek
    Interceding ripples lazily disturb
The grandeur of tranquility on this magic morn

A fantasy of any season of any time
    Dressed in crystals, icicles glistening
Slender prisms in the early light
    Tinkling and winking – blinking
Serene messages sent on this cold yet comfy morn

And still, there's more – for the willow
    In one's dreams is like a snuggled pillow
Bringing calmness to the soul
    From specter to caressing angel
Cradling and held forever on this wondrous morn

Three: We the People

Here we all are, born into the land of our dreams
We are strong of ideas and ideals and so it seems

That all we need to survive is to cherish freedom
And to savor and harbor all who believe in them

We are the people of this country and our being
Strong yet resilient and determined yet willing

To uphold and respect our forefathers' vision
Now revered in our time - our legacy mission

Postscript

This ends the eleventh book of poetry. <u>On On Moving On</u> has been more of a horizontal movement of thoughts. My next book, <u>Up Up and Away</u> will hopefully be a bit loftier and lighter, - a sometime whimsical, sometime inspirational but still an uplifting journey through my time in rhyme. Perhaps known but most times unknown will be these treks into my ever evolving, learning paths of discovery.

See you in the twelfth.

Oh, the whimsy.
Oh, the fun.
Rhyming time is never done."
The Beginning

www.ingramcontent.com/pod-product-compliance
Lightning Source LLC
Chambersburg PA
CBHW052059070526
44584CB00017B/2247